HERTFORDSHIRE LIBRARY SERVICE
WITHDRAWN FOR SALE
PRICE:

Please renew or return items by the date shown on your receipt

www.hertsdirect.org/libraries

Renewals and enquiries: 0300 123 4049

Textphone for hearing impaired: 0300 123 4041

Hertfordshire

ANIMAL
BODY PARTS

BY

Steffi Cavell-Clarke

©2017
Book Life
King's Lynn
Norfolk PE30 4LS

ISBN: 978-1-78637-079-2

All rights reserved
Printed in Malaysia

A catalogue record for this book is available from the British Library.

Written by:
Steffi Cavell-Clarke

Edited by:
Grace Jones

Designed by:
Drue Rintoul

Photocredits
Abbreviations: l-left, r-right, b-bottom, t-top, c-centre, m-middle.

Front Cover tl – Philip Bird LRPS CPAGB. Front Cover tm – Zorandim. Front Cover tr – ChrisVanLennepPhoto. Front Cover br – JONATHAN PLEDGER. Front Cover bm – apple2499. Front Cover bl – Eric Isselee. 2 – john michael evan potter. 4l – Eric Isselee. 4m – isarescheewin. 4r – tanuha2001. 5 – Eduardo Rivero. 6c – Eric Isselee. 6tl – Tsekhmister. 6bl – vblinov. 7t – Daniela_Bethke. 7mt – Przemyslaw Skibinski. 7mb – Rita Kochmarjova. 7b – Volt Collection. 8 – Philip Bird LRPS CPAGB. 9 – stihii. 10 – ChrisVanLennepPhoto. 11 – nattanan726. 12 – Super Prin. 13 – decade3d - anatomy online. 14 – Melory. 15 – mrjo. 15inset – NattapolStudiO. 16 – Leonardo Gonzalez. 17 – wacpan. 18 – Alfredo Maiquez. 19 – Johan Swanepoel. 20 – Eric Isselee. 21 – Donovan van Staden. 22tr – Gepardu. 22c – Emilio100. 22mr – Lyudmila Suvorova. 22tl – Alexandr Makarov 22b – koosen. Images are courtesy of Shutterstock.com. With thanks to Getty Images, Thinkstock Photo and iStockphoto.

CONTENTS

PAGE 4   WHAT IS AN ANIMAL?
PAGE 6   ANIMAL BODY PARTS
PAGE 8   MUSCLES AND BONES
PAGE 10   HEAD
PAGE 12   BODY
PAGE 14   LEGS
PAGE 16   TAIL
PAGE 18   EYES AND EARS
PAGE 20   MOUTH AND NOSE
PAGE 22   LET'S EXPERIMENT!
PAGE 24   GLOSSARY AND INDEX

Words that look like **this** can be found in the glossary on page 24.

WHAT IS AN ANIMAL?

Planet Earth is home to many living things. All living things need water, air and sunlight to grow and survive. Animals, plants and humans are all living things.

A DOG IS A LIVING THING.

A SUNFLOWER IS A LIVING THING.

A BOOK IS A NON-LIVING THING.

Animals live all over planet Earth. There are many different **species** of animal and they all come in many different shapes and sizes. Even though they may look different, many animals share similar body parts.

THERE ARE NEARLY 10,000 NEW SPECIES OF ANIMAL THAT ARE DISCOVERED EACH YEAR.

ANIMAL BODY PARTS

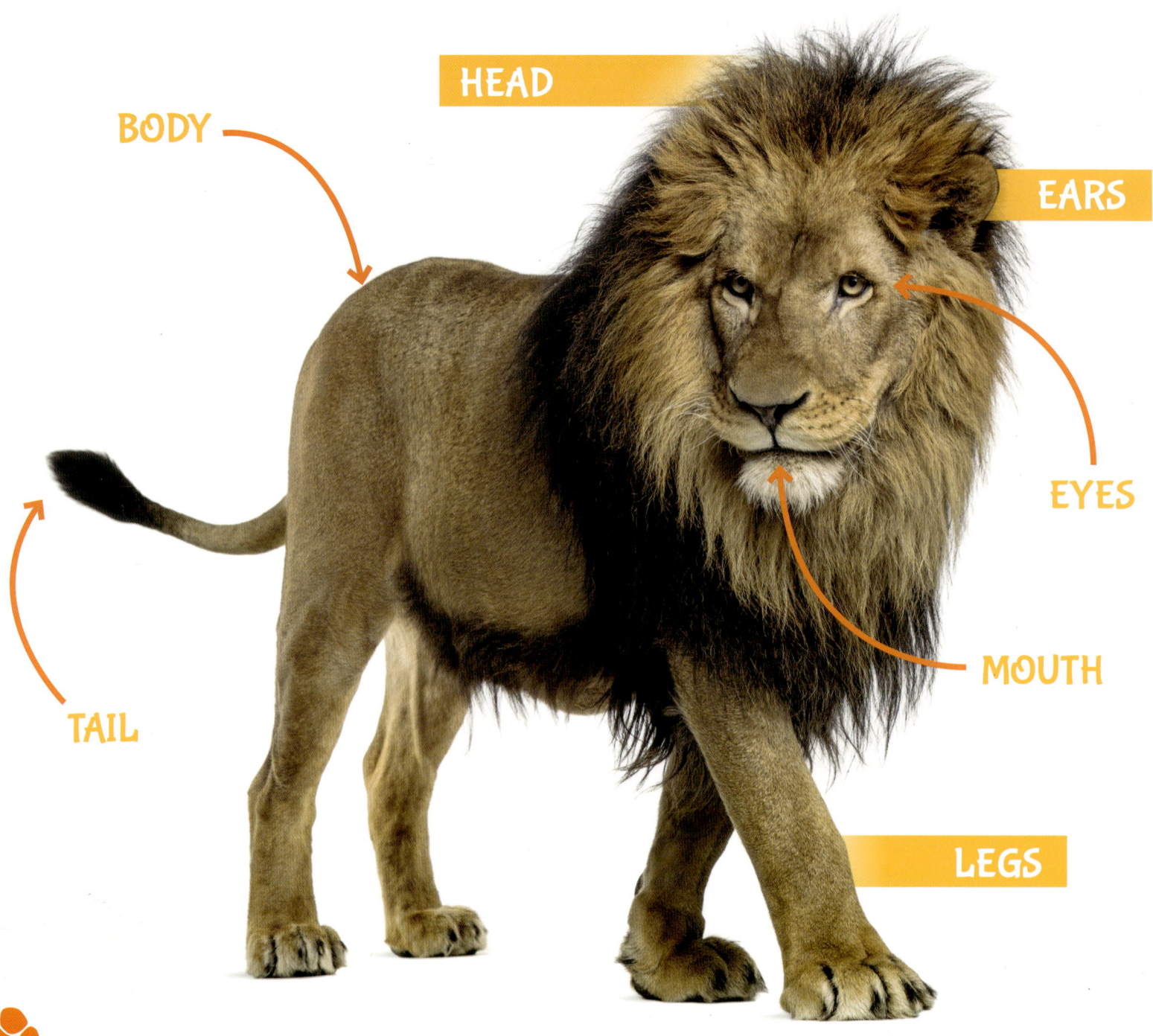

HEAD
BODY
EARS
EYES
MOUTH
TAIL
LEGS

The eyes, nose, mouth and ears are found on the head.

Legs support the body and allow animals to stand, walk and run.

Tails are used for balance.

The body connects all of the other body parts together.

MUSCLES AND BONES

Underneath the skin of an animal there are usually lots of bones and muscles. Many animals are vertebrates, which means they have **backbones**. All the bones connect to make up a **skeleton**.

BIRDS HAVE BONES IN THEIR WINGS TOO!

An animal's body is moved by muscles. Muscles are made up of **body tissue**, which are connected to bones by **tendons**. Animals use their muscles to move the bones in their bodies. Muscles that are used often grow bigger and stronger.

GORILLAS HAVE STRONG AND POWERFUL MUSCLES.

HEAD

Many animals have heads that are connected to the tops of their bodies by their necks. There are some animals that have very long necks, such as giraffes. The head protects an **organ** called the brain.

GIRAFFES HAVE LONG NECKS SO THEY CAN REACH THE LEAVES FOUND ON TALL TREES.

The head is where the eyes, mouth and nose are usually found. Some animals, like fish, have gills near to their heads, which they use to breathe underwater.

NOSE
EYE
MOUTH
GILLS

BODY

The body of an animal is completely covered by skin or **scales**. Animals can also have layers of hair, fur or feathers that grow from their skin, which help to keep their bodies warm.

FEATHERS ALSO HELP BIRDS TO FLY!

Many animals have rib cages, which are groups of bones inside their chests. The rib cage helps to protect important organs, such as the heart. The heart pumps blood around the whole body, which keeps the animal alive.

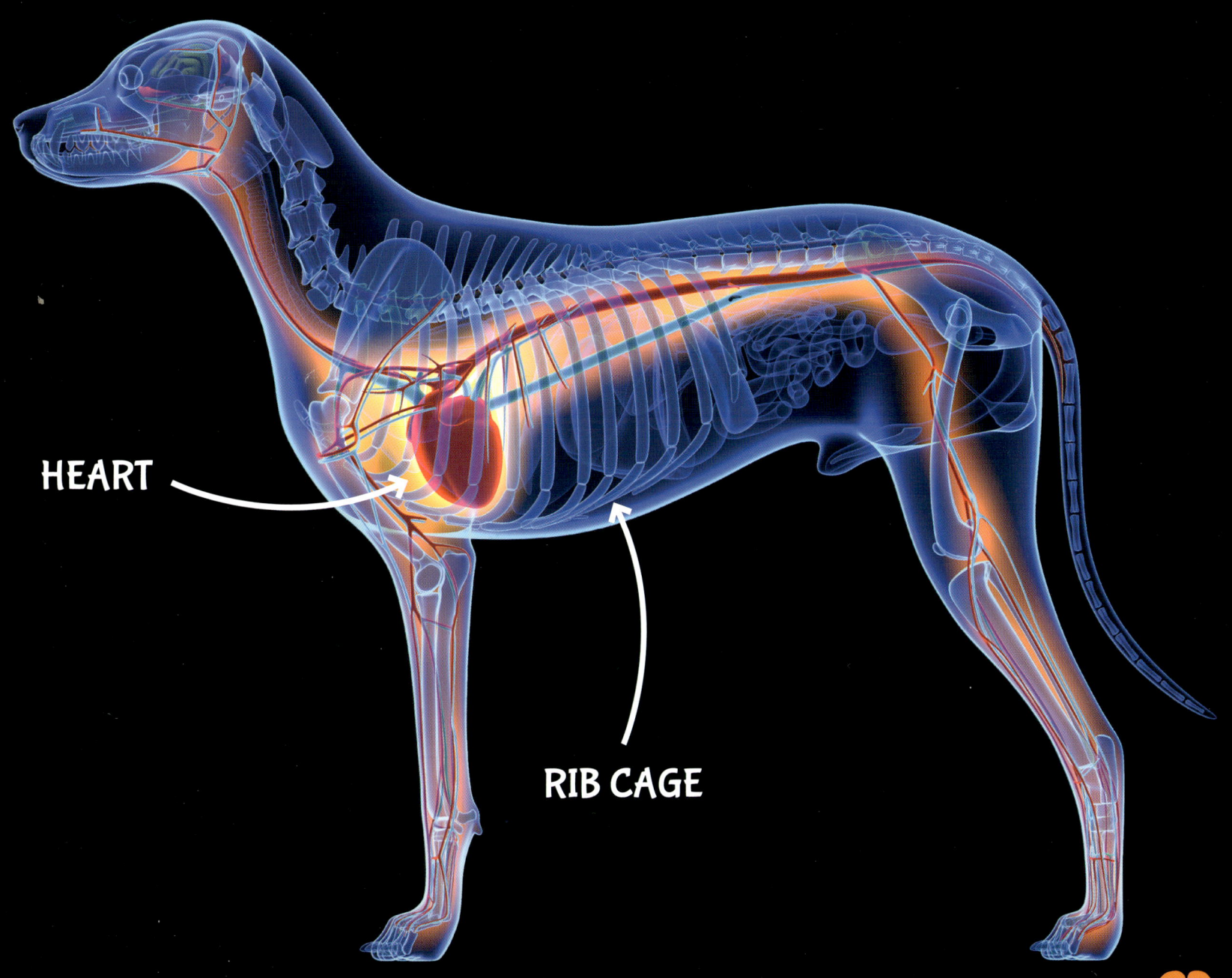

HEART

RIB CAGE

LEGS

KNEE
THIGH
ANKLE
FOOT

Legs are found on the lower part of an animal's body. They are used for moving and to support the body. Legs are made up of bone, muscle and skin. There are many different parts of the leg, including the thigh, knee, ankle and foot.

Some animals do not have any legs at all, like fish and snakes. Snakes use their muscles to move along the ground. Fish have fins that help them to move and change direction underwater.

FINS

TAIL

Many animals have tails, which can be used for many different things. Some animals, such as cats and kangaroos, use their tails to help them to balance. Dogs use their tails for balance too, but they also use them to show how they are feeling; they wag their tails when they are happy!

FISH USE THEIR TAIL FINS TO HELP THEM TO SWIM THROUGH THE WATER.

There are some animals that use their tails to protect themselves against other animals. The scorpion has a stinger at the end of its tail which can release **venom**. When the scorpion is under attack it can flick its tail forward to sting its attacker.

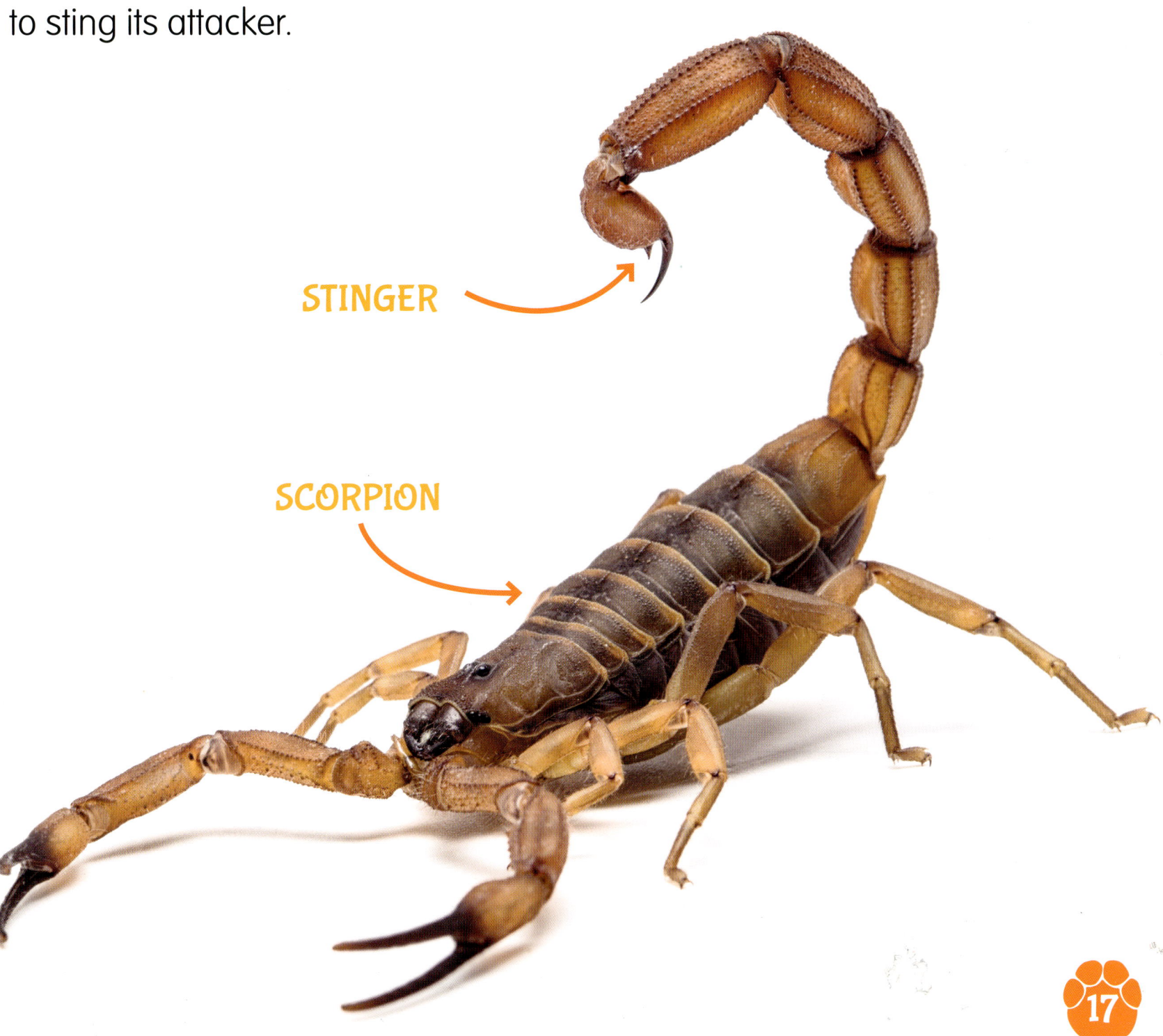

EYES AND EARS

Some animals use their eyes and ears to **sense** the world around them. Most animals need light to be able to see, but there are many **nocturnal** animals that are able to see in the dark, such as owls.

Some animals have small ears that you cannot see. Other animals, like elephants, have very large ears. All animals that have ears use their sense of hearing to listen out for danger.

MOUTH AND NOSE

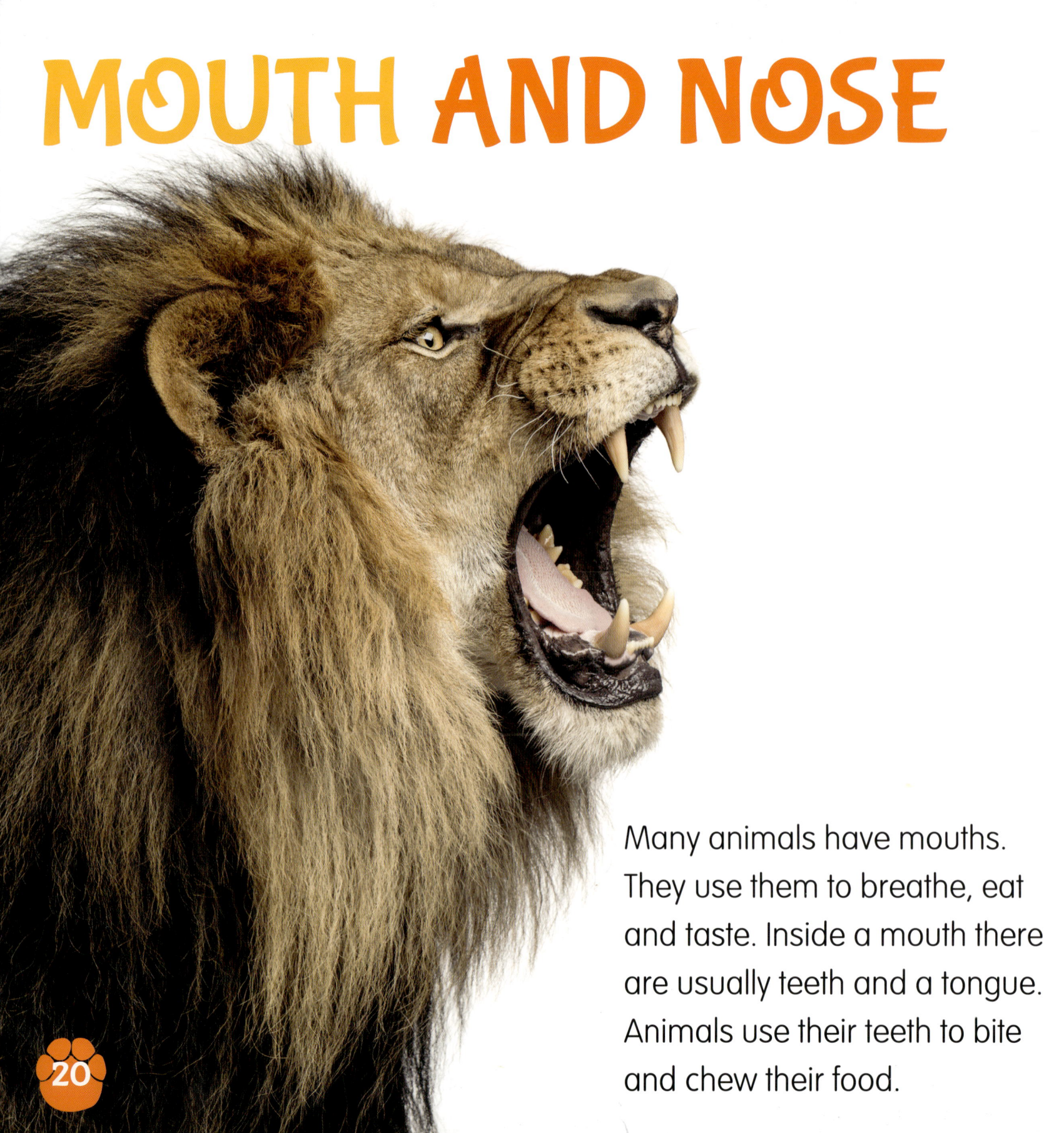

Many animals have mouths. They use them to breathe, eat and taste. Inside a mouth there are usually teeth and a tongue. Animals use their teeth to bite and chew their food.

Lots of animals have noses, which they use to smell. Elephants have very long noses called trunks. They drink by using their trunks to suck up water from rivers and streams.

LET'S EXPERIMENT!

Do you know what body parts a fish has? Let's find out!

You will need:

TISSUE PAPER
GLUE
PIECE OF CARD
CLEAN, USED WASHING UP LIQUID BOTTLE
FELT TIP PENS

TOP TIP
ASK AN ADULT TO HELP YOU!

Step 1

Add pieces of tissue paper to the sides of the bottle for fins.

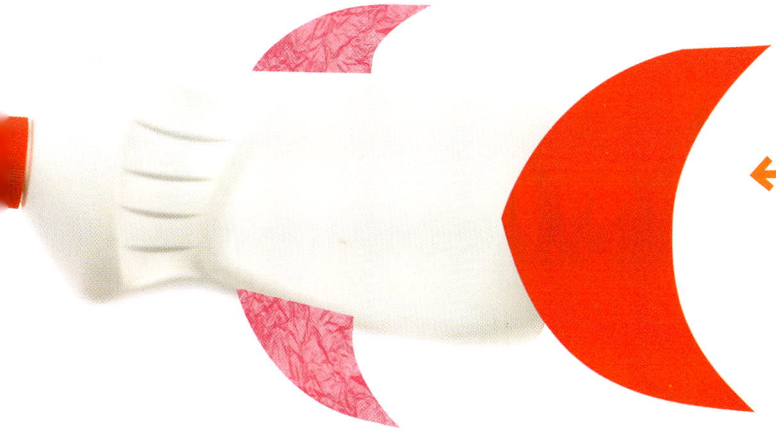

Step 2

Cut out a tail shape from the card and stick it to the bottom of the bottle.

Step 3

Draw on scales over the whole fish.

Draw on gills.

Draw on eyes, a mouth and two small dots for a nose.

Results:

Look at your fish! You have made a fish with its important body parts.

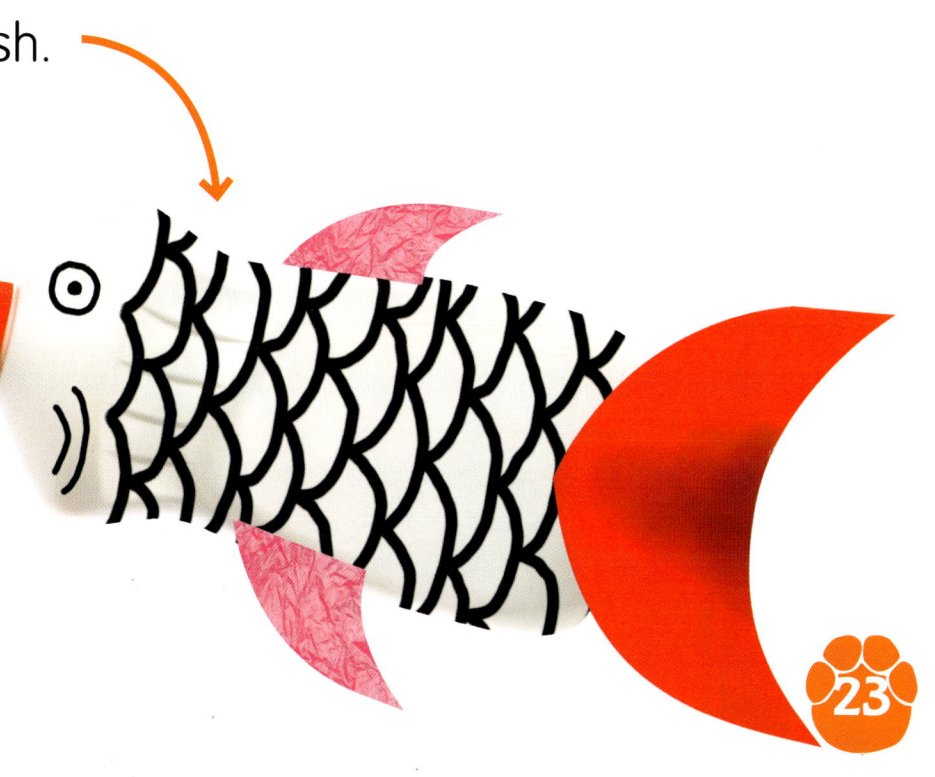

GLOSSARY

backbones — collections of bones in the back, also called spines
body tissue — what organs and other body parts are made of
nocturnal — a living thing that is most active at night
organ — a part of the body that has a particular job to do
scales — small bony plates that protect the skin of a fish or reptile
sense — one of the five senses including sight, smell, touch, taste and hearing
skeleton — frame of bones that support a body
species — a type of animal
tendons — long, stringy cords that join muscles to bones
venom — a poisonous liquid that comes from an animal

INDEX

bones 8–9, 13–14
ears 6–7, 18–19
elephants 19, 21
eyes 6–7, 11, 18, 23
feathers 12
fins 15–16, 23
fish 11, 15–16, 22–23

fur 12
giraffes 10
heads 6–7, 10–11
legs 6–7, 14–15
mouths 6–7, 11, 20, 23
muscles 8–9, 14–15
noses 7, 11, 20–21, 23

scales 12, 23
scorpions 17
senses 18
snakes 15
tails 6–7, 16–17, 23
teeth 20
wings 8